STUFF

You Need To Know To Win A Pub Quiz

Trevor McVeigh

ISBN 13: 978- 1979749695
IBSN 10: 1979749698

Table of Contents

iv

v

Acknowledgements

The Other Team

From left to right: Stuart McKee, Trevor McVeigh, Josie Angell, Gerry Smyth and Billy Gray.

I would like to thank my quiz team (The Other Team) pictured above for all the inspiration and the knowledge I have gathered over the years, by attending various quizzes with them in and around Belfast.

I've appeared in two television quiz shows:

The Link with Billy Gray where we won £5925.

Eggheads with Trevor McVeigh, Stevie McCoo, Billy Gray, Stuart McKee, Gerry Smyth and Tom Nelson but unfortunately we were beat.

Also thanks to Pheme Brown who typed and edited this book, even though she finds all this quizzing malarky a bit boring. So without her this book would not have been possible.

Wedding Anniversary gifts by year U.K

1st Cotton
2nd Paper
3rd Leather
4th Fruit
5th Wood
6th Sugar
7th Wool
8th Salt
9th Copper
10th Tin
15th Crystal
20th China
25th Silver
30th Pearl
35th Coral
40th Ruby
50th Gold
60th Diamond
70th Platinum
80th Oak
85th Wine
90th Granite

Battles

Battle of Naseby 1645

Battle of Culloden 1746

Battle of Lexington 1775

Battle of Waterloo 1815

Battle of Balaclava 1854

Battle of Rorke's Drift 1879

Battle of Gallipoli 1916

Battle of the Somme 1916

Battle of El Alamein 1942

Battle of Goose Green 1982

Battle of Stalingrad 1942

Battle of Bannockburn 1314

Battle of Agincourt 1415

Battle of Yorktown 1781

Battle of the Nile 1798

Battle of Trafalgar 1805

Battle of the Alamo 1836

Battle of Little Big Horn 1876

Battle of Spion Kop 1900

Battle of the Bulge 1945

Battle of Gettysberg 1863

Battle of Bosworth 1485

Star Signs

Aries	March 21st – April 19th
Taurus	April 20th – May 20th
Gemini	May 21st – June 20th
Cancer	June 21st – July 22nd
Leo	July 23rd – August 22nd
Virgo	August 23rd – September 22nd
Libra	September 23rd – October 22nd
Scorpio	October 23rd – November 21st
Sagittarius	November 22nd - December 21st
Capricorn	December 22nd – January 19th
Aquarius	January 20th – February 18th
Pisces	February 19th - March 20th

Super Hero Alter Egos

Batman- Bruce Wayne

Robin – Dick Grayson

Superman – Clark Kent

Supergirl – Linda Lee Danvers

The Flash – Barry Allen

Green Arrow – Oliver McQueen

Green Lantern – Hal Jordan

Thor – Donald Blake

Captain America – Steve Rogers

Mister Fantastic - Reed Richards

The Thing – Ben Grimm

The Invisible woman – Sue Storm

The Human Torch – Johnny Storm

Cyclops – Scott Summers

The Beast – Hank McCoy

The Angel – Warren Worthington III

Iceman – Bobby Drake

Scrabble Tile Values

	Points
A S E N T I L O U R	(1)
D G	(2)
B C M P	(3)
H F V W Y	(4)
K	(5)
J X	(8)
Q Z	(10)

Chinese Zodiac

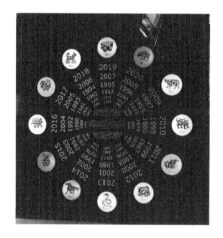

Year of the Rat

Year of the Ox

Year of the Tiger

Year of the Rabbit

Year of the Dragon

Year of the Snake

Year of the Horse

Year of the Goat/Sheep

Year of the Monkey

Year of the Rooster

Year of the Dog

Year of the Pig

15

Comic Characters

Character	Comic
Desperate Dan	Dandy
Lord Snooty	Beano
Dan Dare	Eagle
Alf Tupper	Victor
Keyhole Kate	Dandy
Brassneck	Dandy
Nick Jolly	Hotspur
Morgan the Mighty	Victor
Adam Eterno	Thunder
Robot Archie	Lion
Roy of the Rovers	Tiger
Tricky Dicky	Cor
Beryl the Peril	Topper
I Spy	Sparky
Colonel Blink	Beezer
Desert Island Dick	Topper
Face Ache	Buster
Johnny Cougar	Tiger

British Newspaper Comic Strips

Andy Capp	Daily Mirror/Sunday Mirror
Beau Peep	Daily Star
Ben and Katie	Daily Star
Buck Ryan	Daily Mirror
Clive	Evening Standard
Dick Storey	Daily Express
Flint of the Flying Squad	Daily Express
The Fosdyke Saga	Daily Mirror
Fred Bassett	Daily Mail/ Mail on Sunday
The Gambols	Daily Express/Mail on Sunday
George and Lynne	The Sun
Jane	Daily Mirror
The Larks	Daily Mirror
A Man Called Horace	Daily Mirror/Daily Record
The Perishers	Daily Mirror
Striker	The Sun
Tiffany Jones	Daily Sketch/Daily Mail
Scorcher	The Sun
Rupert Bear	Daily Express

Phobias

Acrophobia	Fear of Heights
Agoraphobia	Fear of Open or Crowded Spaces
Cynophobia	Fear of Dogs
Ophidiophobia	Fear of Snakes
Claustrophobia	Fear of Small Places
Mysophobia	Fear of Germs
Pogophobia	Fear of Beards
Enochiophobia	Fear of Crowds
Trypanophobia	Fear of Needles
Hemophobia	Fear of Blood
Theophobia	Fear of God
Ailurophobia & Gatophobia	Fear of Cats
Globophobia	Fear of Balloons
Philophobia	Fear of Love
Triskaidekaphobia	Fear of Number 13
Lepidopterophobia	Fear of Butterflies
Gynophobia	Fear of Women
Coulrophobia	Fear of Clowns

Horror

The character most often played in films was Dracula.

Lon Chaney's nickname was the Man of 1000 Faces.

Main character in Halloween was Michael Myers.

Main character in Friday 13th was Jason Voorhees.

The killer in the original Friday 13th was Mrs Voorhees.

The name of Stephen King's killer clown was Pennywise.

The rap star who battled Michael Myers was Busta Rhymes.

The name of the hotel in The Shining was The Overlook.

Tubular Bells was the theme from the Exorcist.

The actor buried in his Dracula Cape was Bela Lugosi.

First time a flushing toilet was shown on screen was from Psycho.

The music in Psycho's shower scene was Screaming Violins.

Ghostface's mask in Scream was inspired by an Edvard Munch painting.

Haddonfield, Illinois is the setting for A Nightmare on Elm Street.

Halloween was originally called The Babysitter Murders.

Darts

Study the board and the positions of the numbers.

There are 82 scoring segments on a dartboard.

The lowest number you can't hit with one dart is 23.

Quality dartboards are made from sisal.

The height of the bullseye from the floor is 5 ft 8 inches.

The distance from board to oche is 7ft 9.25 inches.

The first player to achieve a televised 9 darter was John Lowe (1984).

The first player to achieve a live broadcast 9 darter was Shaun Greatbatch (Final of the Dutch Open in 2002).

Phil Taylor has won 16 World Championships, 2 British Darts Organisation and 14 Professional Darts Corporation.

Football Team Nicknames

Addicks	Charlton Athletic
Baggies	West Bromwich Albion
Bees	Brentford
Biscuitmen	Reading
Cherries	Bournemouth
Fosse & Foxes	Leicester City
Hoops	Queen's Park Rangers
Imps	Lincoln City
Irons	West Ham United
Mariners	Grimsby Town
Monkey Hangers	Hartlepool United
O's	Leyton Orient
Pirates	Bristol Rovers
Posh	Peterborough United
Quakers	Darlington
Tics	Wigan Athletic
Tractor Boys	Ipswich Town
Valiants	Portvale
Villains	Aston Villa

Football Grounds

Arsenal	Emirates Stadium
Bournemouth	Vitality Stadium
Burnley	Turf Moor
Hull City	KCOM Stadium
Leicester City	King Power Stadium
Southampton	St Mary's Stadium
Stoke City	Bet 365 Stadium
Sunderland	Stadium of Light
Swansea City	Liberty Stadium
Watford	Vicarage Road
West Ham United	London Stadium
Barnsley	Oakwell
Brentford	Griffin Park
Bristol City	Ashton Gate
Burton Albion	Pirelli Stadium
Derby County	Pride Park
Huddersfield Town	John Smith's Stadium
Preston North End	Deepdale
Rotherham United	Aesseal NY Stadium
Wigan Athletic	D W Stadium

Film Actors Real Names

Jamie Foxx	Eric Bishop
Cary Grant	Archibald Leach
Woody Allen	Allen Konigsberg
Chevy Chase	Cornlius Crane Chase
Ben Kingsley	Krishna Pandit Bhanji
Alan Alda	Alphonso D'Abruzzo
Michael Caine	Maurice Micklewhite
Rock Hudson	Leroy Harold Scherer Jnr
Kirk Douglas	Issur Danielovitch Demsky
Martin Sheen	Ramon Antonio Gerard Estevez
Fred Astaire	Frederick Austerlitz
Michael Keaton	Michael Douglas
Mickey Rooney	Joseph Yule Jnr
Rodney Dangerfield	Jacob Cohen
Charlton Heston	John Charles Carter
Tim Allen	Timothy Allen Dick
Tony Curtis	Bernard Schwartz
Stan Laurel	Arthur Stanley Jefferson
James Garner	James Scott Burngarner

Film Actresses Real Names

Carmen Electra	Tara Leigh Patrick
Demi Moore	Demetria Gene Guynes
Diane Keaton	Diane Hall
Whoopi Goldberg	Caryn Johnson
Joan Crawford	Lucille Lesueur
Judy Garland	Frances Gumm
Elvira	Cassandra Peterson
Marilyn Monroe	Norma Jean Mortenson
Natalie Portman	Natalie Hershlag
Sophia Loren	Sophia Scicolone
Jane Mansfield	Vera Jane Palmer
Jodie Foster	Alicia Christian Foster
Rita Hayworth	Margarita Carmen Cansino
Donna Reed	Donna Belle Mullenger
Kim Novak	Marilyn Pauline Novak
Greta Garbo	Greta Lovisa Gustafsson

Singers Real Names

Courtney Love	Courtney Michelle Harrison
Alicia Keys	Alicia Augello Cook
Shania Twain	Eilleen Regina Edwards
Elton John	Reginald Kenneth Dwight
Katy Perry	Katheryn Elizabeth Hudson
Jessie J	Jessica Ellen Cornish
Calvin Harris	Adam Richard Wiles
Avicii	Tim Bergling
Macklemore	Ben Haggerty
Cee Lo Green	Thomas Decarlo Callaway
Snoop Dog	Calvin Cordozar Broadus
Pink	Alecia Beth Moore
Flo Rida	Tramar Lacel Dillard
Nicki Minaj	Onika Tanya Maraj
Bruno Mars	Peter Gene Hernandez
Slash	Saul Hudson
Bono	Paul David Hewson

The Oscars

The Oscar stands on film reels.

The award weighs 8.5lbs.

The award is 13.5 inches tall.

Due to a metal shortage during World War II, Oscars were made of painted plaster for 3 years.

The first awards were held 16th May 1929.

The first Best Actor Award was Emil Janning.

First person to refuse an award was Dudley Nichols in 1935 (The Informer).

George C Scott was the second person to refuse the award in 1970 (Patton).

Marlon Brando became the third person to refuse an award in 1972 (The Godfather).

First black person to win an Oscar was Hattie McDaniel in 1939 (Gone With The Wind).

When David Nivan was giving his speech in 1974, a streaker ran behind him.

It Happened One Night was the first film to win the big 5 Academy awards, Best Picture, Director, Actor, Actress, and Writing in 1934.

Olympic Games

1896	Athens, Greece
1900	Paris, France
1904	St Louis, USA
1908	London, England
1912	Stockholm, Sweden
1916	Cancelled due to WWI
1920	Antwerp, Belgium
1924	Paris, France
1928	Amsterdam, Holland
1932	Los Angeles, USA
1936	Berlin, Germany
1940	Cancelled due to WWII
1944	Cancelled due to WWII
1948	London, England
1952	Helsinki, Finland
1956	Melbourne, Australia
1960	Rome, Italy
1964	Tokyo, Japan
1968	Mexico City, Mexico
1972	Munich, Germany
1976	Montreal, Canada
1980	Moscow, Soviet Union
1984	Los Angeles, USA
1988	Seoul, South Korea
1992	Barcelona, Spain
1996	Atlanta, USA
2000	Sidney, Australia
2004	Athens, Greece
2008	Beijing, China
2012	London, England
2016	Rio, Brazil
2020	Tokyo, Japan

World Cup Winners

Year	Winner	Host
1930	Uruguay	Uruguay
1934	Italy	Italy
1938	Italy	France
1942 & 1946		Not Held
1950	Uruguay	Brazil
1954	Germany	Switzerland
1958	Brazil	Sweden
1962	Brazil	Chile
1966	England	England
1970	Brazil	Mexico
1974	Germany	Germany
1978	Argentina	Argentina
1982	Italy	Spain
1986	Argentina	Mexico
1990	Germany	Italy
1994	Brazil	USA
1998	France	France
2002	Brazil	South Korea
2006	Italy	Germany
2010	Spain	South Africa
2014	Germany	Brazil
2018	France	Russia

Animal Collective Groups

Alligators	Congregation
Badgers	Set, Cete, Colony or Company
Beavers	Colony or Family
Camels	Caravan, Train or Flock
Cheetahs	Coalition
Dogs	Kennel
Elephants	Herd or Memory
Frogs	Army, Colony or Knot
Lapwings	Deceit
Lizards	Lounge
Porcupines	Prickle
Rattlesnakes	Rhumba
Stingrays	Fever
Tigers	Streak or Ambush
Turkeys	Rafter, Gang or Posse
Thrush	Mutation
Wombats	Wisdom
Woodpeckers	Desent

Baby Animal Names

Alligator	Hatchling
Ant	Antling
Ape	Baby
Camel	Calf
Elephant	Calf
Ferret	Kit
Gorilla	Infant
Hamster	Pup
Jellyfish	Ephyna
Otter	Whelp or Pup
Partridge	Cheeper
Peacock	Pea Chick
Raccoon	Cub
Reindeer	Calf
Skunk	Kit
Spider	Spiderling
Swan	Cygnet or Flapper
Turkey	Poult
Wombat	Joey
Zebra	Colt or Foal
Porcupine	Porcupette

How Many In A Team

Aussie Rules Football	18
Rugby League	13
Rugby Union	15
Polo	4
Water Polo	7
Gaelic Football	15
Shinty	12
Camogie	15
American Football	11
Field Hockey	11
Ice Hockey	6
Netball	7
Basketball	5
Lacrosse	10

Grand National

It first started 1839.

The race is for 7 year olds and up.

Distance 4 miles 514 yards.

There are 30 jumps to make.

First broadcast in 1960.

First winner The Duke in 1836.

Second winner The Duke in 1837

Third winner Sir William in 1838.

The first 3 winners have long been disregarded, as some people believe they took place at Maghull and not Aintree.

In 1928 only 2 finished - Tipperary Tim won at 100/1, Billy Barton fell and remounted for 2nd place.

Foinavon won at 100/1 in1967 after a big pile up.

Red Rum won 1973, 1974 and 1977 and second in 1975 and 1976.

Bob Champion and Aldaniti won in 1981.

The fastest winning time was Mr Frisk at 8m 47.8 secs in 1990.

The Derby

First ran in 1780.

Open to 3 year old colts and fillies.

Race named after the 12th Earl of Derby.

First winner in 1780 was Diomed.

Race was originally 1 mile in 1784.

Changed to current distance of 1 ½ miles.

Lester Piggot is the overall leading jockey with 9 wins, the first was Never Say Die in 1954 and ending with Teenoso in 1983.

Fastest winning time was Workforce in 2010 at 2 minutes 31.33 seconds.

Widest winning margin is 10 lengths by Shergar in 1984.

Anmer was the Kings horse that suffragette Emily Davison threw herself in front of in the 1913 derby, she died from her injuries, Aboyeur won the race at 100/1.

The Derby is part of the Triple Crown which includes the 2000 Guineas and the St Leger.

TV Ads Slogans

Plop Plop Fizz Fizz	Alka Seltzer
Don't Leave Home Without It	American Express
Vorsprung Durch Technik	Audi
The Ultimate Driving Machine	BMW
The World's Favourite Airline	British Airways
A Little Dab'll Do Ya	Brylcreem
Have It Your Way	Burger King
Does She Or Doesn't She	Clairol
It's The Real Thing	Coca Cola
Put A Tiger In Your Tank	Esso
Hand Built By Robots	Fiat Strada
The Best A Man Can Get	Gillette
Snap Crackle Pop	Rice Krispies
Finger Lickin' Good	KFC
Because I'm Worth It	L'Oreal
Good To The Last Drop	Maxwell House
Just Do It	Nike
Does Exactly What It Says On The Tin	Ronseal
The Appliance Of Science	Zanussi

Dr Who

First appeared on the BBC in 1963

The first episode went off 80 seconds late due to extended coverage of President Kennedy's assassination.

The BBC believed many viewers had missed the opening show due to Kennedy's death, so they broadcast it again on 30th November 1963, just before episode 2.

TARDIS = Time And Relative Dimensions In Space.

The Doctors favourite sweets were Jellybabys.

The Doctors planet is Gallifrey.

The Ice Warriors came from Mars.

The 3rd, 4th, and 7th doctor drove a car named Bessie, an Edwardian roadster.

The Weeping Angels are based on the children's game What's the Time Mr Wolf.

Matt Smith is the youngest actor to play the Doctor.

The sonic screwdriver was first used in 1968 by the 2nd Doctor, Patrick Troughton.

Tom Baker, the 4th Doctor played the role for 7 years from 1974 – 1981.

The Doctor is actually is a real Doctor, he studied medicine at Glasgow University, said Patrick Troughton.

The Doctor has 2 hearts.

The Twelve Days of Christmas

One partridge

Two turtle doves

Three french hens

Four calling birds

Five gold rings

Six geese a laying

Seven swans a swimming

Eight maids a milking

Nine ladies dancing

Ten lords a leaping

Eleven pipers piping

Twelve drummers drumming

She gets a total of 364 gifts over the 12 days

Christmas Trivia

Christmas cards started in the UK in 1843 by Sir Henry Cole

Mistletoe berries are white

Christmas crackers were invented by Tom Smith 1847

A snowflake has 6 points

Original 8 reindeer in 1823: Comet, Cupid, Dasher, Dancer, Prancer, Vixen, Donner and Blitzen

Rudolf was added in 1939

Original Santa suit colour was green or tan

Thomas Nast portrayed Santa in red in 1892 for Harpers Weekly magazine

The angel in It's a Wonderful Life was Clarence Odbody

Three Kings Day is A Christian Feast Day better known as The Feast Of The Epiphany

Babbo Natale is Santa Claus in Italy

Joyeux Noel is Merry Christmas in France

Jingle Bells was the first Christmas song played from space in 1965

The cake traditionally eaten in Italy at Christmas is called Panettone

Bada Din is known as Christmas Day in India

Electric Christmas tree lights were invented by Edward Johnson in the U.S.A in 1882

Opening Lines of Books

Call me Ishmael	Moby Dick
It was a bright cold day in April and the clocks were striking 13	1984
It was the best of times It was the worst of times	A Tale of Two Cities
I was born In the year 1632 in the City of York	Robinson Crusoe
You better not never tell anybody but God	The Colour Purple
Last night I dreamt I went to Manderley again	Rebecca
Christmas won't be Christmas without any presents	Little Women
All children except one, grow up	Peter Pan
There was no possibility of taking a walk that day	Jane Eyre
The primroses were over	Watership Down
Marley was dead to begin with	A Christmas Carol
I believe in America	The Godfather

Tag Lines of Films

Check in, unpack, relax, take a shower	Psycho
In space no-one can hear you scream	Alien
You'll believe a man can fly	Superman
Escape or die frying	Chicken Run
They're young, they're in love and they kill people	Bonnie and Clyde
Just when you thought it was safe to go back in the water	Jaws 2
Houston we have a problem	Apollo 13
Be afraid, be very afraid	The Fly
Why so serious	The Dark Knight
They're back	Poltergeist II
Chucky gets lucky	Bride of Chucky
Love is in the hair	There's Something About Mary
The longer you wait the harder it gets	The 40 Year Old Virgin

Classic Literature

Little Women	Louisa May Alcott
Far from the Madding Crowd	Thomas Hardy
Pride and Prejudice	Jane Austin
To Kill a Mockingbird	Harper Lee
The Count of Monte Cristo	Alexandre Dumas
The Great Gatsby	F. Scott Fitzgerald
East of Eden	John Steinbeck
The Catcher in the Rye	J. D. Salinger
Lord of the Flies	William Golding
Gone with the Wind	Margaret Mitchell
Anna Karenina	Leo Tolstoy
Moby Dick	Herman Melville
Uncle Tom's Cabin	Harriet Beecher Stowe
The Colour Purple	Alice Walker
The Mill on the Floss	George Elliott
Cranford	Elizabeth Gaskell
The Woman in White	Wilkie Collins

State Capitals

Alabama	Montgomery
Montana	Helena
Alaska	Juneau
Nebraska	Lincoln
Arizona	Phoenix
Nevada	Carson City
Arkansas	Little Rock
North Carolina	Raleigh
California	Sacramento
North Dakota	Bismarck
Colorado	Denver
New Hampshire	Concorde
Connecticut	Hartford
New Jersey	Trenton
Delaware	Dover
New Mexico	Sante Fe
Florida	Tallahassee
New York	Albany
Georgia	Atlanta
Ohio	Columbus
Hawaii	Honolulu
Oklahoma	Oklahoma City
Idaho	Boise
Oregon	Salem
Illinois	Springfield
Pennsylvania	Harrisburg
Indiana	Indianapolis

State Capitals (cont.)

Iowa	Des Moines
South Carolina	Columbia
Kansas	Topeka
South Dakota	Pierre
Kentucky	Frankfort
Tennessee	Nashville
Louisiana	Baton Rouge
Texas	Austin
Maine	Augusta
Utah	Salt Lake City
Maryland	Annapolis
Vermont	Montpelier
Massachusetts	Boston
Virginia	Richmond
Mitchigan	Lansing
Washington	Olympia
Minnesota	St Paul
West Virginia	Charleston
Mississippi	Jackson
Wisconsin	Madison
Missouri	Jefferson City
Wyoming	Cheyenne

Inventions

Lightning Conductor	Benjamin Franklin
Cats Eyes	Percy Shaw
Jet Engine	Frank Whittle
Television	John Logie Baird
Microwave Oven	Percy Spencer
Submarine	John Philip Holland
Printing Press	Johannes Gutenberg
Mechanical Cash Register	James Ritty
Car Safety Belt	Volvo
Parachute	Louis Sebastien Lenormand
Drinking Straw	Marvin Stone
Tupperware	Earl Silas Tupper
Dishwasher	Josephine Cochrane
Swivel Chair	Thomas Jefferson

What Comes Next In The Sequence

1 – 2 – 5 – 10 – 20	50 (British Coins)
J – A – S – O	N (November)
S – M – H – D – W – M	Y (Year)
R – O – Y – G – B – I	V (Violet)
Y – G – B – B – P	B (Black, snooker balls)
18 – 4 – 13 – 6	10 (Numbers on a dart board)
Brazil, Brazil, England, Brazil, West Germany	Argentina (World Cup Winners)
Roger, John, Brian	Freddie (Members of Queen)
Genesis, Exodis, Leviticus	Numbers (Books of the bible)
Rat, Ox, Tiger	Rabbit (Chinese Years)
Jack, Stan, Roy	Gus (50 ways to leave your lover)

Games

There are More Snakes than Ladders on a Snakes and Ladders Board.

Ludo (Latin for I play).

Guy in jail in Monopoly (Jake the Jailbird).

The policeman in Monopoly (Officer Mallory).

Jenga (Swahili word meaning "to build").

The patient in Operation is Cavity Sam

In Scrabble using all your tiles in one turn is called a Bingo.

There are 42 circles in Connect 4.

Rich uncle Penny bags is the mascot for Monopoly.

The four ghosts in Pacman are Inky, Pinky, Blinky, and Clyde.

Each player has 15 counters at the start of Backgammon.

Subbuteo was invented by Peter Adolph in 1947.

The highest score in the dice game Yahtzee is 5 of a kind worth 50 points and is called a Yahtzee.

Toad Town is the capital of the Mushroom Kingdom, were Mario and Luigi live.

Sherlock Holmes

The first book and film appearance was A Study in Scarlet.

Sherlock's brother was called Mycroft.

Sherlock's address was 221b Baker Street.

Sherlock's landlady was Mrs Hudson.

Sherlock's assistant was Physician John Watson.

Sherlock was killed at the Reichenbach Falls.

In The Adventure of the Empty House, Holmes reappears saying he faked his death.

When Holmes retired he took up beekeeping.

Sherlock used cocaine.

"Elementary my dear Watson" was never said by Holmes in Doyles 60 stories.

The Reichenbach Falls is in the Swiss Alps.

A study in Scarlet was first published in Beetons Christmas Annual in 1887.

There was 56 short stories about Sherlock Holmes written by Sir Arthur Conan Doyle.

Groups Original Names

Van Halen	Rat Salad
Pearl Jam	Mookie Blaylock
Nirvana	Pen Cap Chew
Black Sabbath	Polka Tulk Blues Band
Kiss	Wicked Lester
Coldplay	Star Fish
U2	The Hype
Bare Naked Ladies	Free Beer
Snow Patrol	Polar Bear
Bee Gees	Rattle Snakes
Pink Floyd	The Tea Set
The Who	The High Numbers
10cc	Hot Legs
Slade	Ambrose Slade
Queen	Smile
Simon and Garfunkle	Tom and Jerry
Radiohead	On a Friday
Green Day	Sweet Children
Earth Wind and Fire	The Salty Peppers
Creedence Clearwater Revival	The Gollwogs

6 Wives of Henry VIII

1	Catherine of Aragon	Divorced
2	Anne Boleyn	Beheaded
3	Jane Seymour	Died
4	Anne of Cleves	Divorced
5	Catherine Howard	Beheaded
6	Catherine Parr	Survived

First 7 Beatles and Elvis UK No 1's

Beatles

From Me to You	May 1963
She Loves You	September 1963
I Want to Hold Your Hand	December 1963
Can't Buy Me Love	April 1964
A Hard Day's Night	July 1964
I Feel Fine	December 1964
Ticket to Ride	April 1965

Elvis

All Shook Up	June 1957
Jailhouse Rock	January 1958
I Got Stung/One Night	January 1959
A Fool Such As I	May 1959
It's Now or Never	November 1960
Are You Lonesome Tonight	January 1961
Wooden Heart	March 1961

Pop Trivia Facts

The first CD Album to sell a million was Brothers in Arms (Dire Straits)

The first woman to write and sing a No 1 hit was Kate Bush (Wuthering Heights)

The first digitally produced record was Mirror in the Bathroom (The Beat)

Only palindrome group to have a palindrome hit was Abba (SOS)

The first song played on radio 1 was Flowers in the Rain in 1964

The first group on Top of the Pops was the Rolling Stones (I wanna be your man)

Biggest selling non human No 1 was Bob the Builder

Longest unbroken run at No 1 was Everything I do I do it for you by Bryan Adams (16 weeks)

The most appearances by a group on Top of the Pops was Status Quo with 106.

Led Zeppelin first played Stairway To Heaven live at the Ulster Hall, Belfast, 1971

Al Martino was the first person to have a number one single with Here In My Heart in 1952

World's Air Ports

O'Hare	Chicago
Mehrabad International Airport	Iran
Batman Airport	Turkey
Simon Bolivar International	Venezuela
Fortworth International	Dallas USA
Ronald Reagan	Washington
National Airport	Arlington
Indira Gandhi International	New Delhi
George Bush International	Houston
George Best Belfast City Airport	Belfast
Christoforo Colombo Airport	Genoa
Charles De Gaulle	Paris
Schiphol	Amsterdam
Norman Manley International	Kingston Jamaica
Hartsfield	Atlanta USA

Soaps

Phil Mitchell was shot in 2001 by Lisa Shaw in Eastenders.

Archie Mitchell was murdered by Stacey Branning in 2009 in Eastenders.

Calvin Valentine was shot in 2010 by Theresa McQueen in Hollyoaks.

Tom King was murdered in 2006 by Carl King in Emmerdale.

Frank Foster was murdered in 2012 by Anne Foster in Coronation Street.

Lucy Beale was murdered in 2014 by Bobby Beale in Eastenders.

The first words spoken in Eastenders was "Cor, it stinks in 'ere" by Den Watts.

Minnie Caldwells cat was called Bobby in Coronation Street.

The Rovers racehorse was called Betty's Hot Shot in Coronation Street.

Fred's Folly was a greyhound belonging to Fred Gee and Alf Roberts in Coronation Street.

Peter Barlow has been played by 7 different actors in Coronation Street.

Gilbert was Albert Tatlock's Homing pigeon in Coronation Street.

Saints Days

Saint Valentine 14th February

Saint David 1st March

Saint Patrick 17th March

Saint George 23rd April

Saint Mathias 14th May

Saint Peter 29th June

Saint James 25th July

Saint Bartholomew 24th August

Saint Michael 29th September

Saint Luke 18th October

Saint Andrew 30th November

Saint Stephen 26th December

British Isle Rivers

River Shannon - 240 miles

River Severn - 220 miles

River Thames - 215 miles

River Tyne - 200 miles

River Trent - 185 miles

River Great Ouse - 143 miles

River Wye - 134 miles

River Tay - 117 miles

River Spey - 107 miles

River Bann - 99 miles

River Tweed - 97 miles

River Avon - 96 miles

River Eden - 90 miles

River Dee - 87 miles

River Witham – 82 miles

River Teme – 81 miles

River Don – 80 miles

River Foyle – 80 miles

Cars and Drivers in Wacky Races

Dick Dastardly and Muttley	The Mean Machine
The Slag Brothers	The Boulder Mobile
The Gruesome Twosome	The Creepy Coupe
Professor Pat Pending	The Convert a Car
Penelope Pitstop	The Compact Pussycat
The Red Max	The Crimson Haybailer
Sergeant Blast and Private Meekly	The Army Surplus Special
The Aunt Hill Mob	The Bulletproof Bomb
Lazy Luke and Blubber Bear	The Arkansas Chuggabug
Peter Perfect	The Turbo Terrific
Rufus Ruffcut & Sawtooth	The Buzzwagon

Knights Of The Round Table

There have been various entries of numbers of Knights of the Round Table from 12–150 most people believe these were the Knights of King Arthurs Round Table

Sir Lancelot

Sir Gawain

Sir Geraint

Sir Percival

Sir Boris the Younger

Sir Lamorak

Sir Kay

Sir Gareth

Sir Bedivere

Sir Gahens

Sir Galahad

Sir Tristan

Animals and Their Owners

Duke of Wellington's horse was called Copenhagen.

Napoleon Bonaparte's horse was called Marengo.

Marilyn Monroe had 9 dogs, Most famous was Maf. Hitler's dog was called Blondi.

Laurel and Hardy's dog was called Laughing Gravy.

Winston Churchill's dogs were called Rufus and Rufus II.

Caligula's favourite horse was called Incitatus.

Abraham Lincoln's 2 cats were called Tabby and Dixie.

Bill Clinton's cat was called Socks.

Tonto's horse was called Scout.

Roy Roger's horse was called Trigger.

Ronald Regan's dogs were called Rex and Lucky.

Queen Elizabeth II's favourite horse was called Burmese.

Jesse James's horse was called Red Fox.

Dale Evans's horse was called Buttermilk.

TV Theme Tunes

Programme	Tune
Laurel and Hardy	The cuckoo song
Banana Splits	Tra la la song
Friends	I'll be there for you
The Lone Ranger	William Tell overture
Mash	Suicide is painless
Cheers	Where everybody knows your name
Black Beauty	Galloping home
Alfred Hitchcock	Funeral march of a marionette
Ally McBeal	Searching my soul
The Fall Guy	The unknown stuntman
Father Ted	Songs of love
Monty Pythons Flying Circus	Liberty bell march
University Challenge	College boy
Brush Strokes	Because of you

First 20 USA Presidents

1. George Washington
2. John Adams
3. Thomas Jefferson
4. James Madison
5. James Monroe
6. John Quincy Adams
7. Andrew Jackson
8. Martin Van Buren
9. William H Harrison
10. John Tyler
11. James K Polk
12. Zachary Taylor
13. Millard Fillmore
14. Franklin Pierce
15. James Buchanan
16. Abraham Lincoln
17. Andrew Johnson
18. Ulyses S. Grant
19. Rutherford B. Hayes
20. James A. Garfield

President's Heads on Mount Rushmore

Mount Rushmore is located in the Black Hills of South Dakota, 23 miles southwest of Rapid City in Keystone.

George Washington

Thomas Jefferson

Theodore Roosevelt

Abraham Lincoln

Unveiled 31st October 1941

Height: 18 Metres

Cartoon Trivia

The cat from Pixie and Dixie is Mr Jinks.

Speedy Gonzales is the fastest mouse in all of Mexico.

Speedy Gonzales cousin is Slowpoke Rodriguez (slowest mouse in all of Mexico).

Shaggy from Scooby Doo's real name is Norville Rogers.

Barney Rubble's pet is called Hoppy (a hopparoo).

Fred Flintstone's paperboy is called Arnold.

Homer Simpson's greatest fear is sock puppets.

Mr Magoo's first name is Quincy.

Basil the Great Mouse Detective and Danger Mouse lived in Baker Street.

Popeye has 4 nephews.

Olive Oyl's boyfriend before Popeye was Ham Gravy.

Dino from the Flintstones was a Snorkasaurus.

Mr Magoo's nephew was called Waldo.

Inspector Gadget's niece and sidekick was called Penny.

Count Duckula's butler was called Igor.

Thundercats came from the planet Third Earth.

The Simpsons first featured in the Tracy Ullman show.

The country south of Bedrock in the Flintstones is Mexirock.

Cryptic Clues for Parts
of the Body

(Some of the answers are spelt different, but pronounced the same)

Tug boats do it	Toe
Joins wood together	Nails
Two students	Pupils
Prepare for war	Arm
Top master	Head
Trendy	Hip
Add a P to a famous	
Singer's name	Pelvis
Producer of veal	Calf
A number of negatives	Nose
To do with the sea	Navel
It's not a Rabbit	Hair
You may have one in the cupboard	Skeleton
Doctor in Star Trek	Bones
A child's patella	Kidney

Star Trek

Created by Gene Roddenberry.

TV series started in 1966.

The "T" in James T Kirk stands for Tiberius.

The registry number of the Enterprise is NCC 1701.

Warp drive is powered by dilithium crystals.

First Enterprise captain was Captain Pike.

Mr Spock's blood is green.

Spock's mother was a human teacher from earth called Amanda Grayson.

The first interracial kiss on American network television was on 22nd November 1968 when Captain Kirk kissed Lieutenant Uhura.

Scotty's Christian name was Montgomery.

Star Trek was originally going to be called Wagon Train to the Stars.

In the original draft the Enterprise was called the U.S.S Yorktown.

Captain Kirk commanded a crew of 430.

The last line spoken in the last of the original series was 'If Only'.

The Bible

Methuselah's age at death was 969.

The only 2 people not to die in the Bible were Enoch and Elijah.

Mathias was the disciple who replaced Judas.

John is the shortest book in the New Testament.

After Jesus fed the 5,000, there were 12 baskets of food left over.

Stephen was the first Christian Martyr.

Shem, Ham and Japheth were the sons of Noah.

Jesus first miracle was the turning of water into wine.

Gopher wood was used to build the Ark.

Nimrod was a mighty hunter.

Luke is the longest book of the New Testament.

Methuselah was the son of Enoch, and the grandfather of Noah.

The longest chapter in the Bible is Psalm 119 with 176 verses.

The shortest chapter in the Bible is Psalm 117 with only two verses.

The shortest verse in the Bible is John 11:35 with only two words, " Jesus wept".

Nobel Gases

Helium (He)

Neon (Ne)

Argon (Ar)

Krypton (Kr)

Xenon (Xe)

Radon (Rn)

Atomic Number of Elements

Atomic Number		Symbol
Hydrogen	1	H
Helium	2	He
Lithium	3	Li
Beryllium	4	Be
Boron	5	B
Carbon	6	C
Nitrogen	7	N
Oxygen	8	O
Flurine	9	F
Neon	10	Ne
Sodium	11	Na
Magnesium	12	Mg
Aluminium	13	Al
Silicon	14	Si
Phosphorus	15	P
Sulphur	16	S
Chlorine	17	Cl
Argon	18	Ar
Pottassium	19	K
Calcium	20	Ca

Paintings and Artists

The Last Supper	Leonardo Da Vinci
The Creation of Adam	Michelangelo
Starry Night	Vincent Van Gogh
The Scream	Edvard Munch
Girl With a Pearl Earring	Johannes Vermeer
The Birth of Venus	Sandro Botticelli
Whistler's Mother	James McNeil Whistler
Water Lilies	Claude Monet
The Night Watch	Rembrandt
The Hay Wain	John Constable
The Persistence of Memory	Salvador Dali
Guernica	Pablo Picasso
The Adoration of The Magi	Sandro Boticelli
The Garden of Earthly Delights	Hieronymus Bosch
The Fighting Temeraire	J.M. Turner
Camille - The Woman in a Green Dress	Claude Monet
Transfiguration	Raphael
The Red Vineyard	Vincent Van Gogh

Birth Stones

January	Garnet
February	Amethyst
March	Aquamarine
April	Diamond
May	Emerald
June	Pearl - Alexandrite
July	Ruby
August	Piridot - Sardongx - Spinel
September	Sapphire
October	Tourmaline - Opal
November	Topaz - Citrine
December	Tanzanite - Zircon – Turquoise

Acronyms

N.A.T.O	North Atlantic Treaty Organization
O.P.E.C	Organization of the Petroleum Exporting Countries
N.A.S.A	National Aeronautics and Space Administration
S.W.A.T	Special Weapons And Tactics
U.S.S.R	Union of Soviet Socialist Republic
A.I.D.S	Acquired Imune Deficiency Syndrome
S.D Card	Secure Data Card
M.A.D.D	Mothers Against Drunk Drivers
D.E.R.V	Diesel Engine Road Vehicle
R.A.D.A.R	Radio Detection And Ranging
S.O.N.A.R	Sound Navigation And Ranging
S.I.M Card	Subscriber Identification Module Card
S.M.A.R.T Car	Swatch Mercedes Art Car
S.O.W.E.T.O	South Western Townships
Z.I.P Code	Zone Improvement Plan
S.C.U.B.A	Self Contained Underwater Breathing Aparatus

The New York Boroughs

Manhattan is the home of the Empire State Building and Times Square.

The Bronx is the home of the New York Yankees & Edgar Alan Poe Cottage.

Queens hosts the U.S Open tennis tournament and is home of the New York Mets.

Brooklyn is the most populated of the boroughs with 1,646,000 inhabitants.

Staten Island is the least populated of the boroughs with around 481,000 inhabitants.

General Trivia I

Jane's surname from Edgar Rice Burroughs "Tarzan", was Porter in the book, and Parker in the film.

Antartica is the driest continent on earth, Australia comes second.

The first man made object to break the sound barrier was the whip.

Julius Caesar was stabbed 23 times by his assassins.

The only dog to appear in a Shakespear play was Crab, in Two Gentlemen of Verona.

The Greyhound is the only dog mentioned in the Bible.

Mike Nesmith from the Monkeys mum invented correction fluid in 1956.

The Hardware shop B&Q stands for Block & Quale.

A half multiplied by a half is a quarter.

Kamikaze means divine wind.

Snow White's sister was called Rose Red.

Laurent Blanc was the first person to score a golden goal in a FIFA world cup match.

The TV detective Jim Rockford charged $200 a day plus expenses

The Planets

Mercury

Venus

Earth

Mars

Jupiter

Saturn

Uranus

Neptune

Pluto

Two rhymes to help remember the order of the planets.

My Very Easy Method Just Shows Us Nine Planets.

My Very Educated Mother Just Served Us Nine Pizzas

In 2006, Pluto was reclassified as a dwarf planet, but
that might change again.

Flags

Denmark has the world's oldest flag.

The cedar tree appears on the flag of Lebanon.

Switzerland and the Vatican City have square flags.

Mozambique has a crossed ak47 assault rifle with a bayonet and a hoe.

The flag of the USA has 50 stars and 13 stripes.

Hawaii's state flag is the only U.S state to feature a union jack.

The least used colour in flags is purple.

There are 12 stars in the European flag.

Paraguay is the only country with 2 different sides on it's flag.

Afganistan's flag has been redesigned 20 times, the most by any country.

There are 6 stars on the Australian flag.

The Filipino flag is flown with the red stripe up in the times of war and blue stripe up in times of peace.

Deserts

Deserts	Square miles
Antartica	5,500,000
Artic	5,400,000
Sahara	3,300,000
Arabian	900,000
Gobi	500,000
Kalahari	360,000
Great Victoria	220,000
Patagonian	200,000
Syrian	200,000
Great Basin	190,000
Chihuahuan	175,000
Great Sandy	150,000
Karakum	135,000

Latin Words and Phrases

Ab Irato	From an angry man
Ab Ovo	From the egg
A.D (Anno Domini)	In the year of our Lord
Ad Infinitum	To Infinity
Alibi	Elsewhere
Alma Mater	Nourishing mother
Annus Horribilis	Horrible year
Aqua Vitae	Water of life
Bona Fide	Good faith
Carpe Diem	Seize the day
Cave Canem	Beware of the dog
Caveat Emptor	Let the buyer beware
Compos Mentis	Of sound mind
In Vino Veritas	In wine is truth
Opus Magnum	A great work
Status Quo	Situation in which
Terra Firma	Firm land
Veni Vidi Vici	I came I saw I conquered
Cogito Ergo Sum	I think therefore I am

Mountains

Mount Everest	Nepal
Appalachians	USA
Mount Kilimanjaro	Tanzania
Mount Cook	New Zealand
Pyrenees	France and Spain
Atlas	Morocco, Algeria and Tunisia
Mount Aconcagua	Argentina
Mauna Loa	Hawaii
K2	Pakistan
Mount Logan	Canada
Mount Fuji	Japan
Mount Olympus	Greece
Mount Carrauntoohil	Ireland
Slieve Donard	Northern Ireland
Mount Snowdon	Wales
Mount Mulhacen	Spain
Mount Blanc	France

How Many Sides

Pentagon	5
Hexagon	6
Heptagon	7
Octagon	8
Nonagon	9
Decagon	10
Hendecagon or Undecagon	11
Dodecagon	12
Tridecagon or Triskaidecagon	13
Tetradecagon or Tetrakaidecagon	14
Pentadecagon	15
Icosagon	20
Icosikaipentagon	25
Pentacontagon	50
Hectogon	100

The Wild West

Buffalo Bill's real name was William Frederick Cody.

Dodge City is in Kansas.

Gunfight at the OK Corral was in Tombstone, Arizona.

Doc Holliday was a Doctor of Dentistry.

Jesse James was shot in the back by Bob Ford.

Billy the kid was born Henry McCarty, he was also known as William H Boney.

Sheriff Pat Garrett shot dead Billy the kid in Fort Sumner in 1881.

Calamity Jane's real name was Martha Jane Cannary.

Wild Bill Hickok was shot dead while playing poker, he was holding aces and eights, now known as a dead mans hand and his other card was the Jack of Diamonds.

The last large battle of the U.S. Indian wars occurred in 1890, it was called The Battle of Wounded Knee.

Doc Holliday died of tuberculosis.

Belle Starr was known as the outlaw queen, and was the first woman to be tried by Judge Parker.

Old Measures and Quantities

Palm	3 inches
Hand	4 inches
Span	9 inches
Cubit	Elbow to middle finger tip, approx 18 inches
Rod, Pole or Perch	Approx, 5 1/2 yards
Chain	22 yards
Bolt	40 yards
Furlong	220 yards
League	3 miles
Bakers dozen	13
Score	20
Quire	24 sheets
Gross	12 dozen, 144
Ream	20 quires = 480 sheets

General Trivia II

Benjamin Franklin and George Washington were the first men to appear on postage stamps.

Greta Garbo was known as the face of the century.

The first dollar millionaire in sport was John L Sulivan.

The Rock and Roll Hall of Fame is in Cleveland, Ohio.

The original Apple logo, in 1976 was Isaac Newton sitting under a tree.

Biscuit means twice cooked.

Karate means empty hand.

The circumference of the earth at the equator is around 24,874 miles.

Duncan Black and and Alonzo Decker were the founders of Black and Decker.

Royal Birkdale golf course is located in Southport, Merseyside.

Billy Jean King's maiden name was Moffat.

A unit of heat is a calorie.

The original film the Italian job was set in Turin.

Elvis Presley's first film was Love Me Tender.

U.S State Nicknames

Alaska	The Last Frontier
Arizona	Grand Canyon State
Calafornia	Golden State
Delaware	First State
Georgia	Peach State
Hawaii	Aloha State
Idaho	Gem State
Iowa	Hawkeye State
Kentucky	Bluegrass State
Maryland	Old Line State
Michigan	Great Lakes State
Missouri	Show Me State
Nevada	Silver State
New Jersey	Garden State
Ohio	Buckeye State
Rhode Island	Ocean State
Tennessee	Volunteer State
Washington	Evergreen State
West Virginia	Mountain State
Wisconsin	Badger State
Wyoming	Equality State

List Of Doctor Who Actors

William Hartnell   1963 -1966

Patrick Troughton   1966 - 1969

Jon Pertwee   1970 - 1974

Tom Baker   1974 - 1981

Peter Davison   1982 _ 1984

Colin Baker   1984 - 1986

Sylvester McCoy   1987 - 1989

Paul McGann   1996

Christopher Eccleston   2005

David Tennant   2005 - 2010

Matt Smith   2010 - 2013

Peter Capaldi   2014 - 2017

Jodie Whitaker   2017 - present

Peter Cushing has also played the Doctor in two films

Doctor Who and the Daleks (1965) and Daleks Invasion Earth 2150 (1966)

Lakes

A great way to remember the great lakes, is H.O.M.E S.

- Huron
- Ontario
- Michigan
- Erie
- Superior

Lough Neagh (Northern Ireland) is the largest lake by area in the U.K.

Loch Ness (Scotland) has the largest volume of water in the UK.

Lake Bala is the largest lake in Wales.

Lake Windermere is the largest lake in England.

The Caspian Sea is the world's largest lake.

Lake Superior is the world's largest freshwater lake.

Lake Victoria is the largest lake in Africa.

Original Murder Suspects and Weapons in Cluedo

Miss Scarlett	Candlestick
Colonel Mustard	Dagger
Mrs White	Lead Pipe
Reverend Green	Revolver
Mrs Peacock	Rope
Professor Plum	Spanner
Victim – Dr Black	

First new character introduced since 1949 – Dr Orchid and replaces Mrs White

Planets and Their Moons

There are 181 known moons in our Solar System

Mercury	0 Moons
Venus	0 Moons
Earth	1 Moon
Mars	2 Moons – Phobos and Deimos
Jupiter	67 Moons – Ganymede the largest
Saturn	62 Moons – Titan the largest
Uranus	27 Moons – Titania the largest
Neptune	14 Moons – Tritan the largest
Pluto	5 Moons – Charon the largest

Marx Brothers and Their Movies

Chico, Harpo, Groucho, Zeppo, and Gummo

Humor Risk	1921	never released
The Cocoanuts	1929	
Animal Crackers	1930	
The House that Shadows Built	1931	
Monkey Business	1931	
Horse Feathers	1932	
Duck Soup	1933	
A Night at the Opera	1935	
A Day at the Races	1937	
Room Service	1938	
At the Circus	1939	
Go West	1940	
The Big Store	1941	
A Night in Casablanca	1946	
Love Happy	1949	
The Story of Mankind	1957	
The Incredible Jewel Robbery	1959	

Quiz shows and their Hosts

Double Your Money	Hughie Green
The Bank Job	George Lamb
Bullseye	Jim Bowen
The 21st Question	Gethin Jones
Alphabetical	Jeff Stelling
Sale of the Century	Nicholas Parsons
Rebound	Sean Fletcher
Clever Dicks	Ann Widdecombe
The Code	Matt Allwright
Decimate	Shane Ritchie
Ejector Seat	Andi Peters
Freeze Out	Mark Durden-Smith
The Fuse	Austin Healey
Hive Minds	Fiona Bruce
The Link	Mark Williams
Poker Face	Ant and Dec
Tipping Point	Ben Shepherd
Pressure Pad	John Barrowman

Norse Gods

Odin	Chief God
Frigg	Odin's wife
Balder	Son of Odin and Frigg
Thor	God of thunder and son of Odin and Frigg
Sif	Thor's wife
Loki	Trickster and Odin's adopted son
Sigyn	Loki's wife
Freya	Goddess of love
Bragi	God of eloquence and poetry
Forseti	God of justice
Heimdall	God of light

Greek Gods

Zeus	Chief God, and father of Hercules
Apollo	Son of Zeus
Ares	God of war
Dionysus	God of wine
Hades	God of the dead
Hephaestus	God of fire
Hermes	Messenger of the Gods
Poseidon	God of the sea
Aphrodite	Goddess of fertility, love and beauty
Artemis	Goddess of wildlife
Demeter	Goddess of harvest and fertility
Hera	Queen of the Olympian Gods

Roman Gods

Jupiter	King of the Gods
Pluto	God of the Underworld
Venus	Goddess of Love
Ceres	God of the Harvest
Apollo	God of Music and Medicine
Minerva	Goddess of Wisdom
Diana	Goddess of the Hunt
Mars	God of War
Mercury	Messenger of the Gods
Bachus	God of Wine
Cupid	God of Love
Proserpine	Goddess of the Underworld
Saturn	Youngest son of Uranus, father of Zeus
Vulcan	God of the Forge
Neptune	God of the Sea
Juno	Goddess of Marriage

Egyptian Gods

Amun	King of the Gods, God of the Wind
Amunet	Wife of Amun
Anubis	God of the Dead
Anuket	Goddess of the River Nile
Hapi	God of the River Nile
Horus	God of War, Sky, and Falcons
Isis	God of Magic, Marriage, and Falcons
Khepri	God of Scarab Beetles
Nut	Goddess of Sky and Stars
Osiris	God of the Underworld and Afterlife
Ra	God of the Sun
Serquet	Goddess of Scorpions
Thoth	God of Wisdom and Magic

Pop Hits That Don't Mention the Title in the Song

Annie's song	John Denver
A day in the life	The Beatles
Blue Monday	New Order
Bohemian Rhapsody	Queen
Christmas Wrapping	The Waitresses
Creeque Alley	Mamas and Papas
Iris	The Goo Goo Dolls
Killer	Adamski
Maggie May	Rod Stewart
Ode to Billy Joe	Bobbie Gentry
Paranoid	Black Sabbath
Smells like Teen Spirit	Nirvana
Space Oddity	David Bowie
The ballad of John and Yoko	The Beatles
Unchained Melody	The Righteous Brothers

Alcoholic Cocktails

Blue Hawaii

Rum, Pineapple Juice, Blue Curacao, Sweet and Sour mix and Ice

Cuba Libre

Rum, Coke, Lime, and Ice

Dark and Stormy

Dark Rum, Ginger Beer and Ice

Tequila sunrise

Tequila, Orange Juice, Grenadine, and Orange Wedge

Cosmopolitan

Vodka, Cranberry Juice, Triple Sec, Lime Juice and Ice

Kamikaze

Vodka, Lime Juice, Triple Sec, and Ice

Screwdriver

Vodka, Orange Juice

Sneaky Pete

Rye Whiskey, Milk, Coffee Liqueur, and Ice

B52

Kahlua, Irish Cream, Orange Liqueur

Fuzzy Navel

Peach Schnapps, Crushed Ice, Orange Juice, and Orange Wedge

Thomas the Tank Engine
First Ten Numbers

1   Thomas

2   Edward

3   Henry

4   Gordon

5   James

6   Percy

7   Toby

8   Duck   (real name Montague)

9   Donald

10   Douglas

General Trivia III

Helen Duncan was the last woman to be tried and convicted of witchcraft in 1944.

An inhabitant of Sardinia is called a Sard.

Dreamt is the only word in the English language that ends in MT.

The second full moon in any month is called a blue moon.

Sin City is the nickname of Las Vegas.

Kaiser Chiefs football team come from South Africa.

Terry Wogan was born in Limerick.

Galway is known as the City of Two Tribes.

Spike Milligan's gravestone reads 'I told you I was ill'.

Barbie's sister is called Skipper.

Sindy's boyfriend was called Paul.

Ernest Hemingway had a holiday home in Cuba.

Scafell Pike is located in Cumbria.

Lenin is embalmed in a mausoleum in Red Square.

UK's first surrogate was Kim Cotton.

There are 7 spikes in the Statue of Liberty's crown.

Harry Potter

The four houses in Hogwarts school of Witchcraft and Wizardry are Gryfindor, Ravenclaw, Hufflepuff,and Slytherin.

Students are aged between 11 and 18.

Gringotts bank is ran by goblins.

Harry Potters rival is Draco Malfoy.

There are four goal hoops on a quiddich pitch.

Hagrid's pet dragon was called Norbert.

The golden snitch is worth 150 points.

The spell that wards of Dementors is expecto patronum.

The Daily Prophet is the newspaper that appears most in the movies.

Ginny Weasley keeps a pygmy puff as a pet.

Wizards buy their books at Flourish & Blotts.

Sirius Black is Harry Potters Godfather.

Sybill Trelawney can predict events in tea leaves.

Weasley's Wizard Weezes was the name of the store George and Fred Weasley opened.

Fluffy was the name of the three headed dog.

The Weasley twins are George and Fred.

The Seven Ancient Wonders
Of The World

The Great Pyramid of Giza

The Hanging Gardens of Babylon

The Statue of Zeus at Olympia, Greece

The Temple of Artemis at Ephesus

The Mausoleum at Halicarnassus

The Colossus of Rhodes

The Lighthouse at Alexandria Egypt

The Great Pyramid is the only one of the Ancient
Wonders still standing

Mondays Child

Monday's child is fair of face.

Tuesday's child is full of grace.

Wednesday's child is full of woe.

Thursday's child has far to go.

Friday's child is loving and giving.

Saturday's child works hard for a living.

But the child who is born on the Sabbath day, is bonny and blithe and good and gay.

The Twelve Labours of Hercules

The Nemean Lion

The Lernean Hydra

The Hind of Cerynia

The Erymanthean Boar

The Augean Stables

The Stymphalian Birds

The Cretan Bull

The Horses of Diomedes

The Belt of Hippolyte

The Cattle of Geryon

The Apples of Hesperides

Cerberus

Books and Authors

Roots	Alex Haley
The Colour Purple	Alice Walker
Were Eagles Dare	Alister McClean
A Passage to India	E.M Forster
Gullivers Travels	Johnathan Swift
War and Peace	Leo Tolstoy
Ben Hur	Lewis Wallace
The Count of Monte Cristo	Alexander Dumas
Doctor Zhivago	Boris Pasternak
For Whom the Bell Tolls	Ernest Hemingway
Ivanhoe	Walter Scott
Kidnapped	Robert Louis Stevenson
Les Miserables	Victor Hugo
Paradise Lost	John Milton
Robinson Crusoe	Daniel Defoe
Silas Marner	George Eliot

General Trivia IV

Marilyn Monroe was born with 6 toes on one foot.

Starbucks was named after a character in Moby Dick.

The singular of scampi is scampo.

Sicily is the largest island in the Mediterranean, Sardina is second largest.

Audrey Hepburn was born in Belgium.

The Sunny Isles is off the coast of Scotland.

Pocahontas is buried in Gravesend, Kent.

The U.K National space centre is located in Leicester.

U.N.E.S.C.O   United Nations Educational Scientific and Cultural Organization.

Paul Ince was the first black player to captain England.

Pi = 3.14159265.

Lake Garda is the largest lake in Italy.

Christopher Columbus was born in Genoa, Italy.

Bull's Blood wine comes from Hungary.

The three tunnels in the movie The Great Escape was Tom, Dick, and Harry.

The Ten Largest Objects
In The Solar System

The Sun

Jupiter

Saturn

Uranus

Neptune

Earth

Venus

Mars

Ganymede

Titan

Authors and their Pen Names

Anne Bronte	Acton Bell
Benjamin Franklin	Alice Addertongue, Silence Dogood, Caelia Shortface, Martha Careful & lots more names
Ruth Rendell	Barbara Vine
Charles Dickens	Boz
C.S Forester	Cecil Scott
C.S Lewis	Clive Hamilton
Washington Irving	Diedrich Knickerbocker
Ray Bradbury	Douglas Spaulding
Dr Seuss	Theodor Seuss Geisel
L Frank Baum	Edith Van Dyne
Eric Arthur Blair	George Orwell
Samuel Langhorne Clements	Mark Twain
Stephen King	Richard Bachman
Mary Ann Evans	George Eliot
Charles Lutwidge Dodgson	Lewis Carroll

General Trivia V

Gucci was founded in Florence, Italy.

Andrea Bocelli was formally a court appointed lawyer.

Buddy Holly's Christian name was Charles.

Austin, Texas is known as the live music capitol of the world.

The Royal London yacht club is in Cowes, Isle of Wight.

Four horse racing courses that does not contain the letters R.A.C.E are Huntington, Plumpton, Ludlow, and Goodwood.

Subway is the world's largest fast food chain, with over 40,000 stores.

The indentations on the sides of coins are called reeds.

Stockholm is built on 14 islands.

Elton John's middle name is Hercules.

The opposite of zenith is nadir.

The headquarters of Coca Cola is located in Atlanta, USA .

The church minister in the Simpsons is called Reverend Lovejoy.

Anagrams

Presbyterians

Sway last net them

Woman hitler

Old west action

That great charmer

War on he gets going

Chinchilla reap

Finds a horror

A crap trek twist

Only I can thrill

On any screen

It screams myrrh

Do real filth

Slim alien wrath

Britney Spears

Stanley Mathews

Mother In law

Clint Eastwood

Margaret Thatcher

George Washington

Charlie Chaplin

Harrison Ford

Patrick Stewart

Hillary Clinton

Sean Connery

Merry Christmas

Adolf Hitler

William Shatner

Cryptic Irish Counties

Candles near out	Wicklow
Stopper	Cork
Not feeling good	Down
Banter nothing	Sligo
Power in the north	Tyrone
Insect on the edge	Antrim
Five line poem	Limerick
Not a short crossing	Longford
Not liking friend	Kilkenny
Jonathans not rare	Rosscommon
Nice on chips	Mayo
She is the first lady	Armagh
Increases all the time	Dublin
It's a long way	Tipperary
Sounds like a dog needs one	Laois

Christmas Crackers

The things we do at Christmas

A.N.Y.P	A New Year Party
H.U.T.C.S	Hang Up The Christmas Stocking
K.U.T.M	Kiss Under The Mistletoe
P the C.C	Pull The Christmas Cracker
G.T. the J.S	Go To The January Sales
P.U. the C.T.L	Putting Up The Christmas Tree Lights

Christmas Songs

W.I.the A	Walking In The Air
S.C is C to T	Santa Claus Is Coming To Town
I.D of A, W, C	I'm Dreaming of A White Christmas
W.A.C. is B	When A Child Is Born
I.S.M.K.S.C	I Saw Mommy Kissing Santa Claus
I.B. in F.C	I Believe In Father Christmas

Halloween Horrors Cryptic Clues for Horror Films

A sign	The Omen
I am a doctor, not a monster	Frankenstein
Bad dream on a wooden road	Nightmare On Elm Street
Lone whale (Anagram)	Halloween
Baby's hamlet	Childs Play
The elevations can see	The Hills Have Eyes
Unlucky day	Friday 13th
She is in mourning	The Women In Black
Small toes (Anagram)	Salems Lot
Young child of herb	Rosemary's Baby
Not a day for a contradiction	Night Of The Living Dead
Animal from the dark water	Creature From The Black Lagoon

Cryptic Clues For Musicals

High temperature at the weekend	Saturday Night Fever
Fairground attraction	Carousel
The 20th largest state	Oaklahoma
My spanish mother	Mama Mia
Decorate ones truck	Paint Your Wagon
Sounds like a european country	Grease
Red windmill	Moulin Rouge
Idle medicine man	Doctor Dolittle
You would have to pay to stay here	Holiday Inn
Tale not of the East	West Side Story
Tarzans mate is so clumsy	Calamity Jane
Plasma for the siblings	Blood Brothers
How will we get the baby to sleep	We Will Rock You

Cryptic Clues For Football Teams

Not a woman's meadow	Mansfield
Ships workers	Crewe
Lady Godiva's team	Coventry
Is your mum sick	Motherwell
Only Scottish team mentioned in the Bible	Queen of the South
Always at the front	Leeds
Always a heavy weight	Everton
Build a fortress	Newcastle
Rodney Trotter was named after them	Charlton
Dirty water	Blackpool
Can you hear the prison clock	Celtic
Sparkling home	Crystal Palace
Find them on football boots	Spurs
Is this rock breathing	Livingstone
On top of Ustinov's neck	Peterhead

General Trivia VI

Noddy's friend Big Ears is called White Beard in the U.S.A.

The Marathon is the only athletic event with no world record, but a world's best time.

Red and yellow cards were first introduced in football in 1970.

On Sadie Hawke's Day in the U.S. a women can propose.

Rupert The Bear was the first cartoon strip to appear in a daily newspaper (The Daily Express).

Algeria is the biggest country in Africa.

The highest waterfall in the world is Angel Falls in Venezuela.

The Brooklyn Bridge linking Manhattan and Brooklyn spans the East River.

The names of the 3 Muskateers were Athos, Aramis and Porthos.

The pub in Treasure Island was The Admiral Benbow.

The star Sirius is also known as the Dog Star.

General Trivia VII

The only Shakespeare play with an animal in the title is The Taming of the Shrew.

Bearnaise sauce contains the herb tarragon.

The German Parliament building Reichstag was burnt down in 1932.

Madam Butterfly is set in the Port of Nagasaki.

The drink Ameretto is almond flavoured.

Vesuvius is the only active volcano in mainland Italy (near Naples).

The first Elvis UK no1 hit was All Shook Up in June 1957.

Humphrey Bogart played Charlie Allnut in the film the African Queen.

Robert the Bruce defeated the English at Banockburn.

The piccalo is the smallest member of the flute family.

Captain Nemo captained the submarine the Nautilus.

Ann Nightingale was Radio One's first female DJ.

Oxygen was discovered in 1774 by Joseph Priestly.

A litre of water weighs 1 Kg.

James Bond Films and Title Singers

Dr No	Monty Norman
From Russia with Love	Matt Monroe
Goldfinger	Shirley Bassey
Thunderball	Tom Jones
You Only Live Twice	Nancy Sinatra
On Her Majesty's Secret Service	John Barry (Theme)
Live and Let Die	Wings
The Man With The Golden Gun	Lulu
The Spy Who Loved Me	Carly Simon
For Your Eyes Only	Sheena Easton
Octopussy	Rita Coolidge
A View to a Kill	Duran Duran
The Living Daylights	A-ha
Licence to Kill	Gladys Knight
Goldeneye	Tina Turner
Tomorrow Never Dies	Sheryl Crow
The World Is Not Enough	Garbage
Die Another Day	Madonna
Casino Royal	Chris Cornell
Quantum of Solace	Jack White
Skyfall	Adele
Spectre	Sam Smith

Top Ten Tea Producing Countrys

1	China	1,641,000 metric tons
2	India	967,00 metric tons
3	Kenya	370,000 metric tons
4	Sri Lanka	340,000 metric tons
5	Turkey	231,000 metric tons
6	Vietnam	217,000 metric tons
7	Iran	159,000 metric tons
8	Indonesia	151,00 metric tons
9	Argentina	103,00 metric tons
10	Japan	86,000 metric tons

First 14 Mistermen Characters
(Roger Hargreaves)

1	Mr Tickle	1971
2	Mr Greedy	1971
3	Mr Happy	1971
4	Mr Nosey	1971
5	Mr Sneeze	1971
6	Mr Bump	1971
7	Mr Snow	1971
8	Mr Messy	1972
9	Mr Topsy-Turvy	1972
10	Mr Silly	1972
11	Mr Uppity	1972
12	Mr Small	1972
13	Mr Daydream	1972
14	Mr Forgetful	1972

Astronauts who have walked on the moon

Neil Armstrong	July 1969 (Apollo 11)
Buzz Aldrin	July 1969 (Apollo 11)
Pete Conrad	November 1969 (Apollo 12)
Alan Bean	November 1969 (Apollo 12)
Alan Shepard	February 1971 (Apollo 14)
Edgar Mitchell	February 1971 (Apollo 14)
David Scott	July 1971 (Apollo 15)
James Irwin	July 1971 (Apollo 15)
John Young	April 1972 (Apollo 16)
Charles Duke	April 1972 (Apollo 16)
Eugene (Gene) Ceren	December 1972 (Apollo 17)
Harrison (Jack) Schmitt	December 1972 (Apollo 17)

Afterword

Firstly, I would like to thank you for purchasing my book and secondly I hope you have enjoyed the content and it will help to increase your knowledge for future quizzes.

I have always had the dream of collating the information I have gathered over the years into book form and decided that now was the time to do exactly that.

I am known as a very keen quizzer by my friends and family and I have mustered some useful information over the years. So I hope you have enjoyed reading the book as much as I have in creating it.

I would love to hear any comments/questions you may have about my book (good or bad), as I hope this won't be my last attempt at writing. You can email me on quizfacts@outlook.com and maybe we can exchange our quiz experiences and knowledge.

A note to remember:
As it says on the cover, This is **Stuff You Need To Know To Win A Pub Quiz,** not Mastermind or University Challenge.

Good Luck in your future quizzing and remember - The two secrets of being a good pub quizzer,

Never tell everything you know!!